Rites of Passage™

A Celebration
Of Menarche

Linda M. LaFlamme, M.S.

Moontime™ *Series*

Synchronicity Press

Rites of Passage
A Celebration of Menarche

Published by:
Synchronicity Press
P.O. Box 481• Winchester, MA 01890 USA
(781) 729-3530 • website: http://www.spress.org

Rites of Passage™ and Moontime™ are trademarks of Synchronicity Press.

Printed in the United States of America

Publisher's Cataloging-In-Publication
(Provided by Quality Books, Inc.)
LaFlamme, Linda M.
  Rites of passage : a celebration of menarche / Linda M. LaFlamme — 1st ed.
    p. cm. — (Moontime series)
    Audience: Ages 8-14.
    LCCN: 00-105852
    ISBN: 0-9673449-0-5

    1. Menarche—Miscellanea—Juvenile literature.
  2. Menstruation—Miscellanea—Juvenile literature.
  I. Title.

  RJ145.L34 2001   612.662'08352
                        QBI00-500085

Synchronicity Press

P.O. Box 481
Winchester, MA 01890 USA
(781) 729-3530
website: http://www.spress.org

Grateful acknowledgement is made for permission to reprint excerpts or illustrations from the following copyrighted works:

Women's Bodies, Women's Wisdom by Christiane Northrup, M.D. (Bantam Books, 1994). By permission of Bantam Books.

Special acknowledgement to artist Alice Scott-Moore for her beautiful etching illustrations on pages 17 & 29 and the moon illustration in the journal section.

Also grateful acknowledgement to PSX for permission to use the wonderful illustrations on pages 8, 11, 12, 14 and 35.

Another grateful acknowledgement to Paper Source for permission to reprint the moon illustration on page 15.

Synchronicity Press Books are available at special quantity discounts for bulk purchases for organizations, schools, groups, premiums, fund raising or educational use. Special books or book excerpts can also be created to fit specific needs. For details, write or telephone the office of the Director of Special Programs, Synchronicity Press, P.O. Box 481, Winchester, MA 01890 USA, (781) 729-3530.

To Celebrate and Empower.[sm]

For a Special Girl:

You...

are about to embark on a sacred journey, a beautiful journey from cygnet to swan, from girl to entering womanhood. This is a very special time in your life – so many new ideas, lots of new wisdom and plenty of learning about your changing and blossoming body and soul. You will see that great things are in store for you. And you will discover a whole new dimension of yourself, a beautiful dimension of potential... like a butterfly emerging from a chrysalis.

On this next part of your journey as a young woman you will be discovering more about your inner wisdom and your special and unique qualities, talents and abilities. You will also be learning about the world and about love and compassion – the love that your parents or caregivers have for you, love for others and humanity. And very important, love for yourself. This journey of self-discovery is a life-long process. It is always exciting so relax and enjoy. This is a journey, an adventure and a very special time for you. We honor you and whoever purchased this book for you honors you and your special Rite of Passage.

My Secret

I have a beautiful secret inside. It is a special time... a time for me, a time that I honor. Today I became a woman. Or, should I say I'm becoming a woman. I cherish my secret. And I am eager to watch my secret unfold into a beautiful story.

The Sacred Moon Cycle and the Moon Lodge

Throughout time women's menstrual cycles have been associated with the moon. In certain Native American traditions, women of the tribe went to a special Moon Lodge during menstruation. It was an honorable time of the month for them and meals were brought to them and their household chores were taken care of by others. There they would have a chance to rest and to be introspective—to honor their inner wisdom. Many of the women's cycles coincided with the new moon of the month. In the Moon Lodge, they would rest, meditate, contemplate and receive inspiration.

It was a special and honored time for women, the monthly "moon cycle" or menses. Women became clearer in their visions, dreams, ideas, wisdom and knowledge at this time. After this monthly period of rest, meditation, prayer and dreams, they would bring back to the group their wisdom and insight. The group was grateful and would then incorporate this wisdom.

Use your "moon cycle" well. Include rest and introspection during your monthly menstrual cycle. Pay attention to what you feel, sense and see. And honor your body, mind and soul. Receive your inner guidance and wisdom.

The Door

On walking through the door I see

Someone in the distance... that's me!

So beautiful, smart and poised I appear

And grown up too

But I feel so unsure and new.

How do I get there?

My reflection, gazing lovingly at me,

winked and smiled and said,

"You already have the wisdom inside
of you

...you'll see."

"'Rtu", Sanskrit for "Menses", means "the order and time of the truth".

It also means "season of the year", "light splendor", and it is the name of Vishnu, a Hindu God.

The word "ritual" also comes from Rtu. It also means "any point in time appointed for regular worship".

The order and time of the truth.

Something More

The caterpillar has that knowing inside…
she rests
silently in her cocoon.
She knows that there is
something more…
It's time for the transformation.

One bright day, a butterfly emerges.
Beautiful. Orange, blue and yellow. Free.
She flutters her newborn wings with delight.
She notices another of her kind…
fresh, new
and perfect.

©PSX

Three Generations

I cherish my knowing

Within each cell I will know

the right path.

Like my mother

and grandmother

and all the women before me

across time

I will know.

I honor my womanhood.

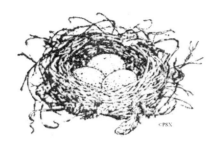

My body

In it's infinite wisdom

Knows the right time

Different Times

We all change at different rates. So don't worry if your friends are ahead of you or behind you. You are all heading in the same direction. And in no time you will all be in the same happy place of knowing.

Today

I hear my younger sister playing.

I could do that if I wanted to

And will sometimes.

But I have other new interests too

On the road to discovery

Friends, dating, my gift to the world,
Me.

What can I see

What can I know

a future bright

I think I'll begin.

About Nature and Your Body

Microcosm and macrocosm. As above, so below.

Everything in the universe consists of cycles...the seasons, the tides, the planets rotating around the sun, the moon, a life.

Scientifically, we can say that the macrocosm (larger unit) is reflected in the microcosm (smaller unit). This is also expressed by the phrase "As above, so below" or even "As in the Heavens, so on Earth".

Moon Phases and Menses

The **new moon** is the dark of the moon, the time when the moon is hidden from view. It is a reflective and introspective time and represents the time of menses. And in fact, some women's menses cycles coincide with the new moon. In legend, it has been said that the moon disappears to her moon lodge at the new moon.

waxing moon – As the moon waxes (appears to be growing or getting larger) it parallels an egg maturing in your ovaries. It is growing and maturing. It is a time of anticipation, building and nurturing.

The *full moon* phase is representative of ovulation, when the egg is fully mature and ready to begin its journey. The full moon is an auspicious time when things in general are said to come to fruition.

waning moon – As the moon wanes (appears to be getting smaller) it enters the stage preparing for the new moon again, just like when your uterine lining is preparing for your menses.

My First Menses

Menarche, or first menses, is a special time for all young women. Find out how others experienced theirs...

— I was so proud that I called all of my friends immediately.

— I was so excited inside. I didn't tell many people, though. It was my own private little secret with my mom and best friend.

—The girls, my friends, celebrated each others...the 4C Club which stood for Christine, Cassie, Carly and Cathy. When one of us started, we would go over to Carly's house, use her parent's good goblet glasses and make a special toast of ginger ale with halved strawberries mixed in for good luck. We each said a nice thing about our friend and then she said something special about us and our friendship and we toasted. It was really a nice sisterhood bonding and we really admired the person who 'got theirs' that we were celebrating.

— In parts of my country we have wonderful celebrations for a girl's first period. We had a ritual and a feast and I was honored also by being given the traditional women's dress to wear for the first time – a recognition and initiation into womanhood. It was beautiful – I shall never forget it.

My Best Girlfriend

We grew up playing
We laughed till we cried
We stayed up late and told stories
and secrets

I'll be there for her
She'll be there for me
There is nothing so special as a true friend.

Your teenage years are filled with such wonderful surprises. It is a time in your life to treasure.
Enjoy, enjoy...

"Happiness is not a station you arrive at, but a manner of traveling."

-Margaret Lee Runbeck

Seasons

Your body experiences the same beautiful and infinite cyclical activity with your menstrual cycle as the Earth does with the cyclical activity of her seasons.

When you begin your menses it is an introspective time like **Winter** with shorter days and the new moon.

As you progress in your new cycle into **Spring**, an egg is maturing like a flower growing and ready to blossom.

Ovulation occurs at the **Summer** point as an egg happily jumps out for its journey down the fallopian tube.

The **Autumn** of your cycle is a reflective time. As the leaves fall off the trees, your body is preparing for your menses so it can begin anew next cycle.

Don't Forget ...

Don't forget that you are unique and special
Don't ever underestimate yourself
Don't give your personal power away
Don't forget to demonstrate
Love and compassion
For your parents and family
And fellow human beings and all creatures
Don't forget that you are deserving
Of love and compassion
Don't forget your friends
Don't be afraid of the dark
Don't be afraid of the light
Don't forget to laugh
Don't override your own wisdom

Do be you.

You can do anything
... be anything.

Today, why don't you take some time
to think about your hopes and
dreams, what you'd like to accomplish
in your youth, how you will get there...

And don't forget to enjoy the journey!

"Dreams are wishes made by the heart."
-*Author Unknown*

Sisterhood

Sisterhood isn't necessarily about bloodlines. It's about understanding the bond between all women on the planet — past, present and future. Sense the oneness, the essence of wisdom, feel compassion and love for all. Embrace women of all ages for you too will go through all of the stages of a woman's life. Honor these stages. And honor the experience and inner guidance of your female wisdom. Sisters unite!

There is nothing so sweet
as the smile from your heart,
dear sister.

Ten Things I Love About Myself

1.

2.

3.

4.

5.

6.

7.

8.

9.

10.

You are wonderful and special. Take some time to realize and remember this and to think about all of the qualities in yourself that make you – You. We hope you realize just how special and unique you are.

Your body is your own
A treasure, a temple
<u>*Always*</u> *know this.*

Encoded Wisdom
of the Female Organs

The Female organs have a symbolic
encoded wisdom.

Menstrual Cycle	Creative cycles and attunement with unconscious lunar information.
Uterus	Creative center in relationship to self.
Ovaries	Creative power in the external world.
Breasts	Giving and receiving nurturing.

* This page excerpt from p. 96 'Women's Bodies, Women's Wisdom by Christiane Northrup, M.D., a book that we highly recommend.

Role Models

I look forward to womanhood. Some of my female role models now are:

Which qualities do they possess that make them role models?

Which qualities might I like to cultivate in myself?

If a role model is a family member or mentor, do you wish to let them know how important and special they are to you? You could send them a note, card or just simply say 'Thank you—I appreciate you! You're very special to me.".

The Looking Glass

I touched the glass
to see – it looked like a reflection of me.

But it was an image
of another sister in the distance
I could see

She smiling at me.

I am not alone
I can feel that in my heart.

And you are not alone, dear sister

I can feel the love and honor that we share

Across miles, across time.
Through the glass.

*B*ecoming a woman is a journey. On this exciting journey, you'll learn about life, yourself and your growing inner wisdom.

Your menses each month is a good time to honor yourself and to connect with this wisdom. Why not start a monthly tradition of your own?

Here are some ideas:

- Take 1/2 day to be good to yourself
- Explore career options
- Have a delicious, healthy, nourishing meal of your favorite foods
- Take a relaxing herbal bath
- Do research on something that interest you
- Write in your journal
- Give yourself a manicure, pedicure or facial
- Spend an hour in nature – a park, by a lake, in your backyard
- Go out with your friends
- Get dressed up
- Learn something new
- Breathe… just be
- Try a new hobby
- Do one kind deed unasked, expecting nothing in return
- Read a new book
- Take 15 minutes to meditate
- Laugh a little, tell a joke, laugh a lot
- Dream big

What can I do as a monthly treat for myself?

Make a list below or in your journal of some fun and healthy ideas that you can do just for yourself each month. These can be healthy and fun -physically, intellectually or emotionally. After you have made your list, choose one (or two) and treat yourself each month. Make a commitment to your list and to your health and happiness!

_____

_____

_____

_____

_____

_____

_____

_____

_____

The Perfect Me

We come in all shapes and sizes — curvy, athletic, muscular, short, tall, skinny and round. Know that you are perfect just the way you are!

Be perfect—be <u>you</u>!

My Interests

Which subjects, careers, hobbies, dreams, paths or ideas interest you? What might you wish to learn more about? List them below. You can then make a plan to do research at the library, at a computer, borrow or buy a book, or even plan to take a class. Maybe you could speak with others in that field or even join a club...

Look Inside, Follow your Heart, Find your Passion...

My Work in the World

Which career opportunities might you wish to explore? Let your imagination soar and list them below.

_____

_____

_____

_____

_____

_____

_____

_____

_____

_____

"This above all:
To thine own self be true."
-From Shakespeare's 'Hamlet'

Gratitude

Gratitude is a very special feeling to cultivate and to experience. According to Webster's Dictionary, it is "the state of being grateful, a warm and friendly feeling toward a benefactor, the kindness awakened by a favor received, or thankfulness". It benefits you most of all because, according to ancient wisdom, "you get back what you give". Why not take some time, set aside a minute or two each night and think of something that you are thankful for. Feel appreciation for this. How has this person, place, thing, deed, act, situation enriched your life? Feel gratitude in your heart. You can start a list or journal even of all that you are grateful for. You may want to start with The Gratitude Page on the next page in this book and you may continue in your journal

Gratitude is silently remembering and thanking those who have enriched your life – be it from a small act of kindness to a large deed or for a happy memory. And, of course, you need not be silent about it. Be as loud as you want!

"I praise loudly,
I blame softly."
—Catherine II of Russia

The Gratitude Page

I am grateful for…

1 _____

2 _____

3 _____

4 _____

5 _____

6 _____

7 _____

8 _____

9 _____

10 _____

11 _____

12 _____

13 _____

14 _____

15 _____

Moontime™
Menarche Personal Cycle Charts

Your very own Menarche Personal Cycle Charts are on the following pages so that you may record the date that you received your first period and plan when you will receive it in the future.

Moontime™
Menarche Personal Cycle Charts

You can use the Menarche Personal Cycle Charts on the following pages to record the date that you receive your first period and to plan when you will receive it again the following month. After a few months of tracking with the charts you may see patterns and may predict with more accuracy your own personal cycle – in how many days can you expect it, how long does it usually last, which days are heavier than others and so on. Some women also like to record the way they feel or any other significant happenings. Is there a pattern? Others find it fun to also record the moon phases and see how their menses relates to that. Simply fill in the name of and dates of the month. Then mark the date you begin your period. You may also note other characteristics like heavy or light (relating to flow). Choose your own symbol for marking Day 1. Some women choose a heart, a flower or something creative. Or you may simply mark an x. To plan when you will receive your next period, count from Day 1 of your last period to the next expected date. Remember, everyone's cycle is unique – there may be an average of 28 days but that doesn't mean that more or less isn't normal – everyone is different. And you should honor that and your own body's uniqueness. After you begin to see a pattern, you can feel more comfortable in knowing when to expect it and have awareness of your cycle. Please see sample for ideas. Good luck Sister!

S a m p l e C h a r t

Month: <u>November</u>

Sun	Mo	Tue	We	Thu	Fri	Sat
	1	2	3	4	5	6
7	8 ● new moon	9	10 ♥ light	11 ♥ heavy	12 ♥ med	13 ♥ light
14 ♥ light	15	16	17	18	19	20
21	22	23 ○ full moon	24	25	26	27
28	29	30				

You can customize and use the following charts to record your first six months of menses. Additional Personal Cycle Charts are available- see website or back of book.

Month: _____

Su	Mo	Tu	We	Th	Fri	Sat

Month: _____

Su	Mo	Tu	We	Th	Fri	Sat

Month: _____

Su	Mo	Tu	We	Th	Fri	Sat

Month: _____

Su	Mo	Tu	We	Th	Fri	Sat

Month: _____

Su	Mo	Tu	We	Th	Fri	Sat

Month: _____

Su	Mo	Tu	We	Th	Fri	Sat

My Menarche Journal

❀❀❀❀❀❀❀❀❀❀

Use the following pages as a private journal to record your very own thoughts of this special time, your Menarche. You can also continue with your journal monthly and you may also want to record any ideas, thoughts, dreams, or changes as you experience them.

Congratulations Sister, you're on your way!

I am not afraid of storms,
for I am learning how to sail my ship.
-Louisa May Alcott

Keep company with those who make you better.
-English Saying

A light heart lives long.
-William Shakespeare

No man is worth your tears.
And the one who is will never make you cry.
-Author Unknown

Truth is the most valuable thing we have.
-Mark Twain

Then the time came when the risk it took
To remain tight in a bud
Was more painful than the risk it took to blossom
-Anais Nin

*The future belongs to those who believe
in the beauty of their dreams.*
-Eleanor Roosevelt

Courage is resistance to fear, mastery of fear-
Not absence of fear.
-Mark Twain

Carpe Diem
Seize the day!

The only way to have a friend is to be one.
-Ralph Waldo Emerson

Real knowledge is to know the extent of one's ignorance.
-Confucius

The best and most beautiful things in the world cannot be seen or even touched—they must be felt with the heart.
-Helen Keller

Argue for your limitations and sure enough they are yours.
-Author unknown

We are what we repeatedly do.
-Aristotle

People are just about as happy as they make up their minds to be.
-Abraham Lincoln

No one can make you feel inferior without your consent.
-Eleanor Roosevelt

_And life is what we make it.
Always has been, always will be.
-Grandma Moses_

It is good to have an end to journey toward;
But it is the journey that matters, in the end.
-Ursula K. Le Guin

Surround yourself with only people
who are going to lift you higher.
-Oprah Winfrey

As long as you're going to be thinking anyway, think big.
-Donald Trump

We all live with the objective of being happy;
our lives are all different and yet the same.
-Anne Frank

If you refuse to accept anything but the best,
you'll get the best. Begin to live as you wish to live.
-Author Unknown

I have learned from experience that the greater part of our happiness or misery depends on our dispositions and not on our circumstances.
-Martha Washington

Do you have a story to contribute to the next edition of this book? Do you have any ideas, suggestions or comments? We welcome your input and would love to hear from you.

Please direct comments or stories to: **Synchronicity Press** at the address in the front or by email at info@spress.org Or please visit our website at http://www.spress.org

We hope that you enjoyed this celebration book!

Do you have a story to contribute to the next edition of this book? Do you have any ideas, suggestions or comments? We welcome your input and would love to hear from you.

Please direct comments or stories to: **Synchronicity Press** at the address in the front or by email at info@spress.org Or please visit our website at http://www.spress.org

We hope that you enjoyed this celebration book!

Synchronicity Press

Books and Products:

Moontime™ *Series*

- **Rites of Passage**™ **A Celebration of Menarche** Gift Book $19.95
- **Rites of Passage**™ **Moontime**™ Gift Set* $24.95
- **Moontime**™ **Journal** $12.95
- **Celebrating Her Special Event,** Adult Companion Booklet to Rites of Passage *-Free w/Rites of Passage Gift Set*
- **Reconnecting with our Cycles, Connecting with Ourselves** $12.95 *A healing cultural and personal exploration of the emotional, esoteric, physical, symbolic and spiritual aspects of menses.*
- **Moontime**™ **Personal Cycle Charts** $4.00
- **Moontime**™ **Gift Card** $2.00
- **The Adventures of Clara T., Menses Girl**™ *Humorous and fun comic-style book* $5.95
- **Wisdomia, Menopause Woman**™ *Witty comic-style book* $5.95

*Gift Set includes Rites of Passage Gift Book, Celebrating Her Special Event, Moontime™ *Personal Cycle Charts and Moontime*™ *Gift Card.*

To Celebrate and Empower.ˢᵐ
Visit us at http://www.spress.org

Synchronicity Press

Quick Order Form

Fax orders: 781-721-7306. Send this form.

Telephone orders: Call 1-800-845-6828 toll free. Have your credit card ready.

Email orders: info@spress.org or visit http://www.spress.org

Postal orders: Synchronicity Press, P.O. Box 481, Winchester, MA 01890, USA

-Books/product list on reverse-

Please send the following books/products. I understand that I may return any of them for a full refund—for any reason, no questions asked.

_____

_____

_____

_____

Please send me more FREE information on:

Other books   Seminars   Affiliate Program   Celebration Events

Name:_____

Address:_____

City_____ State_____ Zip_____

Telephone_____

Email address:_____

Sales tax: Please add 5% for products shipped to MA addresses.

Shipping by air: US: $4.50 for the first item and only $2 for each additional book.

International: $9 for first item; $4 for each additional book (estimate)

Payment: Check   Money Order   Visa   Mastercard

Card Number:_____

Name on card:_____ Exp. Date:___/___

Signature: _____

Synchronicity Press donates a portion of its profits to charity. Your purchases benefit not only the next generation of women but other worthwhile causes too!

*Tell your friends... tell your sisters... celebrate women.... celebrate life!*ˢᵐ

Synchronicity Press

Books and Products:

Moontime™ *Series*

- **Rites of Passage**™ **A Celebration of Menarche**
  Gift Book $19.95
- **Rites of Passage**™ **Moontime**™ **Gift Set*** $24.95
- **Moontime**™ **Journal** $12.95
- **Celebrating Her Special Event,** Adult Companion Booklet to Rites of Passage -*Free w/Rites of Passage Gift Set*
- **Reconnecting with our Cycles, Connecting with Ourselves** $12.95 *A healing cultural and personal exploration of the emotional, esoteric, physical, symbolic and spiritual aspects of menses.*
- **Moontime**™ **Personal Cycle Charts** $4.00
- **Moontime**™ **Gift Card** $2.00
- **The Adventures of Clara T., Menses Girl**™ *Humorous and fun comic-style book* $5.95
- **Wisdomia, Menopause Woman**™ *Witty comic-style book* $5.95

*Gift Set includes Rites of Passage Gift Book, Celebrating Her Special Event, Moontime™ *Personal Cycle Charts and Moontime*™ *Gift Card.*

To Celebrate and Empower.^{sm}
Visit us at http://www.spress.org

Synchronicity Press

Quick Order Form

Fax orders: 781-721-7306. Send this form.

Telephone orders: Call 1-800-845-6828 toll free. Have your credit card ready.

Email orders: info@spress.org or visit http://www.spress.org

Postal orders: Synchronicity Press, P.O. Box 481, Winchester, MA 01890, USA

-Books/product list on reverse-

Please send the following books/products. I understand that I may return any of them for a full refund—for any reason, no questions asked.

_____

_____

_____

_____

Please send me more FREE information on:

Other books   Seminars   Affiliate Program   Celebration Events

Name:_____

Address:_____

City_____ State_____ Zip_____

Telephone_____

Email address:_____

Sales tax: Please add 5% for products shipped to MA addresses.

Shipping by air: US: $4.50 for the first item and only $2 for each additional book.

International: $9 for first item; $4 for each additional book (estimate)

Payment: Check   Money Order   Visa   Mastercard

Card Number:_____

Name on card:_____ Exp. Date:___/___

Signature: _____

Synchronicity Press donates a portion of its profits to charity. Your purchases benefit not only the next generation of women but other worthwhile causes too!

*Tell your friends... tell your sisters... celebrate women.... celebrate life!*sm

Synchronicity Press

Books and Products:

Moontime™ *Series*

- **Rites of Passage**™ **A Celebration of Menarche**
  Gift Book $19.95
- **Rites of Passage**™ **Moontime**™ **Gift Set*** $24.95
- **Moontime**™ **Journal** $12.95
- **Celebrating Her Special Event,** Adult Companion Booklet to Rites of Passage *-Free w/Rites of Passage Gift Set*
- **Reconnecting with our Cycles, Connecting with Ourselves** $12.95 *A healing cultural and personal exploration of the emotional, esoteric, physical, symbolic and spiritual aspects of menses.*
- **Moontime**™ **Personal Cycle Charts** $4.00
- **Moontime**™ **Gift Card** $2.00
- **The Adventures of Clara T., Menses Girl**™ *Humorous and fun comic-style book* $5.95
- **Wisdomia, Menopause Woman**™ *Witty comic-style book* $5.95

*Gift Set includes Rites of Passage Gift Book, Celebrating Her Special Event, Moontime™ Personal Cycle Charts and Moontime™ Gift Card.

To Celebrate and Empower.℠
Visit us at http://www.spress.org

Synchronicity Press

Quick Order Form

Fax orders: 781-721-7306. Send this form.

Telephone orders: Call 1-800-845-6828 toll free. Have your credit card ready.

Email orders: info@spress.org or visit http://www.spress.org

Postal orders: Synchronicity Press, P.O. Box 481, Winchester, MA 01890, USA

-Books/product list on reverse-

Please send the following books/products. I understand that I may return any of them for a full refund—for any reason, no questions asked.

_____

_____

_____

_____

Please send me more FREE information on:

Other books   Seminars   Affiliate Program   Celebration Events

Name:_____

Address:_____

City_____ State_____ Zip_____

Telephone_____

Email address:_____

Sales tax: Please add 5% for products shipped to MA addresses.

Shipping by air: US: $4.50 for the first item and only $2 for each additional book.

International: $9 for first item; $4 for each additional book (estimate)

Payment: Check   Money Order   Visa   Mastercard

Card Number:_____

Name on card:_____ Exp. Date:___/___

Signature: _____

Synchronicity Press donates a portion of its profits to charity. Your purchases benefit not only the next generation of women but other worthwhile causes too!

*Tell your friends... tell your sisters... celebrate women.... celebrate life!*ˢᵐ

Synchronicity Press

Books and Products:

Moontime™ *Series*

- **Rites of Passage™ A Celebration of Menarche** Gift Book $19.95
- **Rites of Passage™ Moontime™ Gift Set*** $24.95
- **Moontime™ Journal** $12.95
- **Celebrating Her Special Event,** Adult Companion Booklet to Rites of Passage -*Free w/Rites of Passage Gift Set*
- **Reconnecting with our Cycles, Connecting with Ourselves** $12.95 *A healing cultural and personal exploration of the emotional, esoteric, physical, symbolic and spiritual aspects of menses.*
- **Moontime™ Personal Cycle Charts** $4.00
- **Moontime™ Gift Card** $2.00
- **The Adventures of Clara T., Menses Girl™** *Humorous and fun comic-style book* $5.95
- **Wisdomia, Menopause Woman™** *Witty comic-style book* $5.95

*Gift Set includes Rites of Passage Gift Book, Celebrating Her Special Event, Moontime™ Personal Cycle Charts and Moontime™ Gift Card.

To Celebrate and Empower.℠
Visit us at http://www.spress.org

Synchronicity Press

Quick Order Form

Fax orders: 781-721-7306. Send this form.

Telephone orders: Call 1-800-845-6828 toll free. Have your credit card ready.

Email orders: info@spress.org or visit http://www.spress.org

Postal orders: Synchronicity Press, P.O. Box 481, Winchester, MA 01890, USA

-Books/product list on reverse-

Please send the following books/products. I understand that I may return any of them for a full refund—for any reason, no questions asked.

_____

_____

_____

_____

Please send me more FREE information on:

Other books   Seminars   Affiliate Program   Celebration Events

Name:_____

Address:_____

City_____ State_____ Zip_____

Telephone_____

Email address:_____

Sales tax: Please add 5% for products shipped to MA addresses.
Shipping by air: US: $4.50 for the first item and only $2 for each additional book.
International: $9 for first item; $4 for each additional book (estimate)

Payment: Check   Money Order   Visa   Mastercard

Card Number:_____

Name on card:_____ Exp. Date:___ /___
Signature: _____

Synchronicity Press donates a portion of its profits to charity. Your purchases benefit not only the next generation of women but other worthwhile causes too!

Tell your friends... tell your sisters... celebrate women.... celebrate life!